SEEKING BYLAND

For my parents
Shirley and Allen Johns

Seeking Byland

*Poems through the Seasons
from Stanbrook Abbey*

Laurentia Johns, OSB

Foreword by Bishop Hugh Gilbert, OSB

GRACEWING

First published in England in 2020
by
Gracewing
2 Southern Avenue
Leominster
Herefordshire HR6 0QF
United Kingdom

www.gracewing.co.uk

Translation of Extracts from *Geni Crist*, by Madog ap Gwallter,
© 2020, Laurentia Johns, OSB

ISBN 978 085244 965 3

Typeset by Word and Page, Chester, UK

Cover design by Bernardita Peña Hurtado

Front cover image: Byland Abbey, North Yorkshire
(David Armitage)

CONTENTS

ACKNOWLEDGEMENTS

Acknowledgements are due to the editors of following publications where some of these poems, versions and the translation of 'Geni Crist' (p. 2) have appeared: CAFOD; *The Tablet*; *Religious Life Review*; *Spirituality,* and *Theology.*

'Viaticum: A Paschal Villanelle' (p. 42), written in memory of Dylan Thomas (1914–53), echoes that poet's villanelle 'Do not go gentle into that good night', first published in *Botteghe Oscure*, VIII, p. 208, in November 1951, and which appeared as no. 69 in Thomas's *Collected Poems* (London: Dent, November 1952).

'Mary Reflects' (p. 19) was commissioned by St Matthew's Church, Northampton, Christmas 2017. Their support is much appreciated.

Thanks are due to Dr Iestyn Daniel, Dr Caroline Yeates and Dom Teilo Rees, OCSO, for help with the translation of *Geni Crist*, 'The Birth of Christ' (p. 2).

Any mistakes or infelicities are those of the translator.

I am deeply grateful to the many friends who have encouraged me to persevere in the poetry furrow over the years, and would like to record particular gratitude to those who have helped nurture this collection:

Sheila Johns, Richard Jones and Aelred McColm, OSB. Special thanks go to Will Franklin for invaluable technical assistance.

Lastly, I am indebted to Tom Longford and all at Gracewing for their professional expertise and patience.

Laurentia Johns, OSB
Stanbrook Abbey, August 2020

FOREWORD

In his 1858 essay on the Mission of St Benedict, St John Henry Newman describes the monastic life as 'poetical'. Never greatly expanding on his meaning, he has left some readers perplexed, nuns and monks included. Surely, though—he might have said—a life lived in rural surroundings, in step with the seasons, and shaped by the feasts, fasts and ferias of the Church's year and the psalms and hymnody of her daily prayer may well engender a mode of seeing, clear-eyed and sacramental, that may find a natural expression in poetry. Perhaps it is indicative that St Hilda, a Benedictine nun (of Yorkshire!), thanks to her nurturing of Cædmon, can be claimed as the mother of English poetry.

There are many secret and subtle compatibilities between the making of verse and the living of the monastic life - not least in both being things we need, unobtrusively vital. How much darker the world would be without either of them!

These poems are blessedly free of the first person singular, which is why they refresh. They are located in place, set in time and connected to things. They stabilise and slow us. They are shapely and slender, like glasses holding an aperitif. They are not afraid of unexpected juxtapositions, the quirky even, but peace, as Newman would say, 'is the very air they breathe'. They see traces of the Resurrection in heaped leaves and other unlikely places, and so proffer hope as irrepressibly as a life of prayer.

It is good they are being brought together and published here. Some lives have already been enhanced by them; now the circle will expand. They confirm Newman's intuition about the Benedictine 'mission', and in their self-effacing way they are an epiphany of the Spirit:

> stabling us to bear gifts,
> to journey through nights,
> to pay
> homage even to small things:
> to trust stars. (Pentecost)

May many turn their eyes and ears to them.

Bishop Hugh Gilbert, OSB
Feast of the Exaltation of the Holy Cross, 2020

ix

Alchemy

Silver birch
a wand
of wax
showers
golden sparks
to ground
vestiges
of Autumn past
and makes
the land
a lighted torch
a path of flames
to mark the way
this Advent

'The Birth of Christ'

Extracts from *Geni Crist*, by Madog ap Gwallter, fl. *c.* 1250

A Son has been given us,
a birth felicitous,
a favoured Son,

a Son Glorious,
a Son to redeem us,
a Son peerless.

Son of a virgin mother
of sweet piety,
mature in speech,

With no natural father,
this is the gracious Son,
bestower of blessings ...

Tiny colossus,
strong, mighty, frail,
of pale cheeks,

Wealthy and needy,
our Father and Brother,
author of judgements:

This is Jesus
whom we hail
King of Kings,

Lowly and lofty,
Emmanuel,
heart's honey ...

Desiring no silks,
no white stuffs
for swaddling bands;

Instead of fine
linens, rags
decked his crib ...

To speak to shepherds,
watchers of flocks,
there came

Angel hosts,
and night became
bright as day.

Then were declared
and believed
joyful tidings:

The very birth
of God, yes, in the
City of David ...

Christmas Night:
night like no
baneful nights,

A night of gladness
for all Christians:
may it be so for us!

The Envoy

There it was,
luminous
in the western sky,
presiding gently,
as new-borns
do. A slender crescent,
slightly tilted,
as if to pour out grace:
cradled nine full moons,
now sent
to rock the world.

Star Cross

In the star we see the cross
its points, the thorns,
the azure ring, his robe.
The light which shines on all,
the arms which embrace all.

And this despite their mockery,
mock majesty, pageant pantomime and pomp.
All human conceptions of kingship
border on the vaudeville,
verge on the burlesque.

Kings in a stable
out of proportion,
distorted, like the body on the cross,
our attempt to nail down Divinity.
Racked and disjointed,
still suffering our mock homage.

Cast crowns, cast lots, cast off your
tawdry kind of kingship,
so much dressing up,
Christ rides triumphant over cast-down cloaks,
every inch a king with none of the apparel.
His crown, the star
the Cross, his throne where he
invests the cosmos with his gift
of Love, unadorned.

The Herald

This star burns
like the bush.
Call it a comet
portentous,
pointing beyond itself:
Behold the Lamb of God.
This star, unlike the bush,
dies as it burns.
A trail-blazer,
drawing kings,
changing hearts,
it fades:
He must increase, I must decrease,
falls back to earth,
burned out in mission,
the world alight.

Epiphanytide

pulsing Christmas light inland,
  riding Spring's extending fetch,
   wave upon wave, inching forward
      slowly as Somme
     yet ever gaining ground,
      each swash and backwash
        sure and relentless
        as lengthening days,
        widening the kingdom,
         breaching all darkness,
          promising fullness
          and merciful rest.

Baptism

This is a land
of quiet wonders:
of soil-creep and
freeze-thaw,
overflow channels,
reverse drainage;
things weren't as they are.

This is terrain
that has witnessed marvels:
glaciers melting,
fountains of stone,
boulders re-sited,
waves high as mountains,
sheer cliffs transformed.

Here streams run as strangers,
misfits in valleys
not of their shaping,
lost in a largeness
which renders them free.
Likewise the exiles,
new-born in baptism,
journey in hope
through a land not their own
yet as wide as the sea.

Cana Sky

Pale watery sky
brimful of day
catches ablaze
so the guests
gasp and stay
fixed in a trance
as a fine Beaujolais
bright as a dance
melts grey away
She requests
You amaze
day after day
Cana sky

Divine Stratagem

'Be reasonable, God—
it will never work. It hardly
holds on paper: that thin stem
and delicate, drooping head,
more spirit than flesh—
but in the real world?
Consider what it's up against:
earth hardened by frost,
cutting North winds,
driving rain.
To proceed would be naïve. Besides,
it will never get past your
Botanical Advisers.
They know you must be strong.
No one wins with little white flowers—
however exquisite.'

'My people need them.
They are weary of Winter.
Long enough their eyes have
fasted on bleak greys and paleness.
I will break them in gently—
plain food after sickness—
too early yet for the rich
Spring hues. For now let my
white suffice. Let them feast on
these pearls of great price,
treasure the field of my mercy
and glimpse, in hidden hallmark,
the secret sign of my strength.'

Snowdrops at Wass

Diminutive

miniatures

of themselves

as if painted

with pointed tip

on china cups

pearly as

egg shells

and as

perfectly

formed

Spring's Vanguard

Spring's vanguard,
seeded for glory,
mustered today
on verge and village green:
gently swaying pennants,
proclaiming, even now,
Christ's victory.

Snow at Candlemas

Is fitting, right,
the shining white
for cleansing,
a tongue of searing flame,
prolonging Christmas
into Winter's grey,
extending newness
with each lengthening day.

The hush, the silence
of the lamb for slaughter,
the pause surrounding
ancient Sarah's laughter
filled here with stillness:
Simeon and Anna.

The cold, the chill
of death's dark vale,
an avenue of mourning,
now pierced by Christ's own light,
becomes a passageway
to glory.

After the Thaw

And so the ground's appeared
—green, if not dry—
which forty days has lain
under the wintry deep:

                              an Advent Lent.

The land looks frail
as a limb freed
from a cast, needing
air and sunlight:

                              convalescent.

There swoops the raven
while the absent dove
bids us step out
—faintly at first—
to seek her tokens
on this new-born,
sodden, fragile earth:

                              hope is not spent.

God's Conundrum

I wonder, God said,
how to re-kindle wonder?

Like lichen it grew in the Garden
unnoticed yet adding zest,
spangled dew of Eden
on mossy banks,
freely given sheaves
of beauty—everywhere.

Then, heedless, they ate
and, eyes wide open,
saw only trees,
a soviet sameness
of grey, tangled branches
and, of course,
the now needed fig leaves.

God thought:
I must set a tree ablaze ...
Attract them with marvels ...

And from the wine-red whips
of Winter willow, there rose
a holy conflagration—
and somebody noticed.

Moses,
the man to lead God's
people back to wonder ubiquitous,
to Paradise Surpassed, to
Jesus.

Behold the Man

They may have looked alike;
he did not know,
he could not see.
But the paste felt good
and the voice sounded
deep inside.

He went—no sticks—
straight to Siloam,
propelled
by a new force.
He stooped, and sensed
the cool breath of the pool
then cupped his hands,
inclined his head,
and leant into the deep,
as if in homage.

He stumbled back,
more faltering than before,
blinded by light
and pulsing shades.
He lost his sense of earth.
Then, still far off,
he saw the Temple
glinting in the sun,
and men like trees,
gesticulating.

As he approached
—he saw it plain—
they were not pleased
to see him.
The questions rained
on him like fists; parents denied
him. He spoke two simple words:

'I am.'

Two words, two witnesses,
enough to put a man
to death, or to expel him.
He found him at the pool,
gazing into the depths
which bore two faces,
blurred by rippling light:
image and likeness met.

He turned
and knew him then
before he spoke.
He closed his eyes,
now seeing clearly.
He knelt; the earth smelt good.
He kissed the dust,
and understood.

Twilight Sonata

Above,
a wedge of day,
pushes south
against increasing night
as if to keep ajar
the door to hope.
This shining slope,
made up, they say,
of particles of dust
lit up from afar
points back to that
primal stellar birth.

Below,
on Earth,
a glow-lit path,
a moonglade of daffodils,
plays in the dark
ghost-notes of light.

Mary Reflects

It was and it wasn't a light.

I looked up with a start
from the spinning wheel
mantled in sunshine:
no shadow was cast
as the tip of a wing brushed past.

It was and it wasn't a voice.

I sensed it to be at the good
Lord's behest that his
messenger made this
bizarre request that he would
be my guest.

It was and it wasn't a fright.

I trembled yet thrilled
and knew in my heart
there was something right,
something willed
from all time in this tryst.

It was and it wasn't a choice.

Though I didn't know why—
and how even less—
how could I, in the face
of such great gentleness,
not say 'Yes'?

A Spring Hailstorm

In memoriam M.L.H., 2011-2015

It was sudden,
this hail, shrouding Spring
fields white as pain;
a shock, a sting,
Winter again?

No, rather,
hope reborn;
a clean shift;
newness;
a fresh leaf
—on blackthorn—
turning
history's drift
with a word we could not
guess:
this maiden's, simple, shining, solid

'Yes.'

Lily-Crucifix

As moon to earth,
and even pre-birth,
their orbits mesh:
synchronised breathing
God's *nephesh.*
Her silver light lunar
to his solar gold
yet each one
eclipsed
this Lady Day's noon
by the other's 'Yes',
fiat voluntas tua.
Never closer than this,
never further from death:
two lives without parallax,
wedded—strange bliss—
on a flowering Cross:
Lily-Crucifix

Rite of Spring

And then, onto this almost
finished canvas
flew swallows,
as if to dot the 'i' and cross
the 't' of victory,
your finished symphony.
What do they bring
to this rite of Spring
that hasn't now been said
in the Father's serene brightness,
and the Son's new greenness?
Perhaps, the Holy Spirit's quickness
that marks the difference
'twixt living and dead.

O Buzzard

Sky-clad rider
of clouds,
you make the rook
look like a flapper,
so effortless
your graceful,
silent glide; fanned
wings spanning
unmarked arcs
as if to describe
stately circuits
of kings
or the soul's
wide orbit

Maundy Daffodils

All felled, the daffodils,
felled, like Hopkins' poplars.
They were lovely as Jerusalem in Spring,
floating gold on green, pointing
heavenwards.
Now felled, cast down on the ground
like a crumpled ball gown,
strewn petals of taffeta,
a love all spent.

To what does this point,
beyond tricks of weather?
When we gaze at these flowers,
what do they say?

They mime desolation
as vast as the ocean,
fading fragments of glory,
a sepia estate;
outrageous reversals,
a mass floral grave.

Some struggle, half fallen,
to play, as they used to,
quartets in a wasteland,
the pulse of a dance.

But there, by the cedar,
untouched by the storm,
stands God's Pietà:
one single bloom,

keeping Love's vigil
through his darkest night,
till bloodstained battle-
gear is burnt,
and 'history is steeped in light'.

No Need for a Sign

A bowl of daffodils on the sanctuary,
as if sprung from some hidden, central source,
explodes in a haze of angled gold.

Is this an acceptable offering,
love's libation singing praise in silence?
Reflected glory of your presence?

These blooms, like cantilevered
cantors, truly listen,
strain to hear the golden
sounds they shape.

They almost seem to descant
on buttressed
greenness which bears,
invisibly,
the weight of grace.

Fall in Spring

Oaks look, in early Spring,
already autumnal:
leaves, frail as a foetus
perfectly formed yet set
in garlands of rusting gold,
seem to shrivel softly
as a dislodged chrysalis,
recalling the death encased
in all created flesh.

This semi-dirge, tuned out
by full-throttled thrushes
and scrambled by the screaming green,
we almost fail to hear
but deep within the fear
persists:
yes,
we are mortal.

Cadentine Rites

A Sequence for Holy Week

Palm Sunday

A pre-dawn mist hovers
over the Severn, as at the start,
while above, anticipatory, hangs
that rose-glow herald of day,
a Rothko block of pink,
pierced by a single fleck
of light, almost unseen:
the morning star,
a weak and fading pointer
to this week's end
where light will be eclipsed.

Why this Waste?

Day two and everything to do:
worlds to create
liturgies to plan.
Enter the profligate
balm-bearer, breaching every mean,
the water of her tears below
their stream of words: a vault between.
They're earth and sky apart, and yet,
he takes his cue from her:
his name is oil poured out,
from him shall waters flow.

On the Third Day

The cock faces south but Spring
sun can't be trusted.
There's betrayal in the air.
This third day should bring
resurrection, but not
without death. Must it be so?
No chance to avert melt-down?
Need we bend to inevitable sin?
It could be quite different.

Yet ...
This is the day God wrested land
from oceans—a forceful birth—
growth shooting from separation.
Those seeds imply loss,
and one of them fathered the Cross.

Feria Quarta

Night has fallen.
Bring on the luminaries,
those who govern day and night,
who mark times and festivals:
Caiaphas and Pilate.
One speaks the truth
unknowingly,
one speaks to Truth
unknown, while
Truth himself shines silently.

Cadentine Rites

Dawn's chorus breaks the silence:
rooks tumble, a chiff-chaff saws;
still life fills with animation,
throbs with the pulse of our High Priest
who celebrates cadentine rites,
stoops to wash feet,
pours out his words, his life,
intones the Great Hallel
and leads us out
across the Kedron brook
into his mysteries.

'Cadentine', a neologism pronounced to rhyme with Tridentine, suggests a descending action or motion (cf. Latin *cadere*, 'to fall').

Very Good Friday?

Today should be the climax:
God's viceroy and creation's crown.
Instead, what have we done?
Crowned him with thorns,
decked him with wounds,
and crucified upon the wood
our brother, God's own Son.
(Are we his keeper?)
To see this day as 'good'
needs eyes piercing as Balaam's,
a heart as pure as John's.
For most of us, it looks like death,
and can't be understood
except as finished.

Not Finished but Accomplished

God rested on the Sabbath day
his work complete:
a sketched first draft
which worked on paper
but proved unviable
faced with mortal resistance.
And so began the toilsome task
of teaching us the truth
of love unlimited.

The waters broke late
in this death-birth
strange baptism,
breaching nature's way,
but now Christ rests,
his long labour over
and stillness hovers
above the earth
as at the first.

The Eighth Day

God speaks again
—and not in repetition—
the first, a sending,
now, a calling back.
He says:
'Let there be Light,'
and the Son,
obedient,
rises, glorious
as seven noons in one.
This day will have no night.
It bids us
follow Christ above
to enter and to rest
in bright communion:
the overflowing consciousness
of Love.

Seeking Byland

They said from here
you can see Byland.

I never could,
though I stood
nodding quasi-sagely
as arms flailed vaguely
south towards some
medieval pile
at quite a distance:
I knew it wasn't that.

They said wait for the
Winter. You'll see it then;
no leaves to block the view.

I never did, despite
peering through gaps,
scanning for something new;
no, I found it not.

Then, unsought, on Easter morning,
it was just there,
larger than life and hazily majestic,
like a tall ship beached in a wood
or a wreck rising from a sea fret.

So clear—how could you miss it?
So near, you might have touched it.
Was this a vision? Easter faith?

By noon, it had vanished from sight,
lost in shadow, the other side of light.

'A hart can never . . .'

A dawn-lit deer—
a doe, a hind, a hart?
stood there with no hint of fear,
fawn against Easter green,
questioning this building in its field.
A steep-backed silhouette,
A slim frame,
charged with latent
strength in the tensed hind parts
as if to scale the air,
turned instead and met
my wondering stare
with eyes innocent
as Eden: I felt forgiven.

He is Risen

I went seeking Byland
but found instead
two deer leaping—
twin alleluias—
full of grace and
almost asking:
'Why seek the living
among the dead?'

She is Risen

Skyward you swung
censers of golden
glory: a daffodil fanfare
to raise the dead.
Today you laced
blossom of blackthorn
through hedgerow tresses,
as for a lover's head;
and from the new hawthorn,
shouted, rather than said:
'She is risen!'

Viaticum: A Paschal Villanelle

In memoriam Dylan Marlais Thomas, 1914-1953

Christ did go gently into that dark night.
He made it good, turned it to day:
his goodness heals our mortal blight.

When close friends scattered, driven by fright,
leaving him as evil's prey,
Christ did go gently into that dark night.

Religious men thought it was right
to turn him in, to have their way.
His goodness heals our mortal blight.

Headlong, he faced full Roman might,
despite the taunts, their cruel play,
Christ did go gently into that dark night.

Though squads of angels were there to fight,
he chose rather to trust and pray;
his goodness heals our mortal blight.

Yet one small figure flickered bright
whose standing presence helped him stay:
so Christ went gently into that dark night;
his goodness heals our mortal blight.

Wass Peacock: An Ascension Shewing

'Raising up the penniless from the ground and the poor
from the dung-heap, to set them among royalty.'

First came the sound:
a muffled clicking
of feather
on bone; the knitting
together
of spirit and flesh:
Ezekiel's vision.

Then came the view,
a Julian shewing:
long pinions unfurling
'neath a mastering blue
of the Father's favour,
Christ's Church:
no single colour
but a seemly blending,
all shades a-shimmer,
translucent, full:
amplitude,
plenitude,
this feast of eyes:
a royal pavilion,
true tent of meeting:
an ascension in deed.

Pentecost

The Spirit's Epiphany
        making us kings,
    stabling us to bear gifts,
            to journey through nights,
         to pay
homage even to small things:

to trust stars.

Poppies

Just burst
the pods reveal
scarlet
tightly packed
as a clenched fist
spilling out like
parachute
silk

Open petals
unmask
caldera pools
like eyes
blood-red, kohl-black,
streaked, as if weeping all war.

Selfheal

(Prunella vulgaris)

In memoriam Helen Griffin, d. 29 June 2018

'Not a better wounde herbe in the world'
John Gerard, sixteenth-century herbalist

Selfheal
leaves suppliant
stem skybound
purple head
striving
to the sun
God's collaborator
not even semi-
pelagian
this tiny
wild flower
thriving
only at his touch
becomes for us
a healing plant
a panacea

New Wine

Effervescent
elderflower,
intricate
fragrant
simple,
in you, heaven
condenses
a vast
constellation:
lacy
heady
bridal,
arousing the
senses, awaking
the soul: Summer's
corsage; an earnest
of Autumn's
vintage,
and the Kingdom's
new wine

Not even Solomon

All flesh is grass ...
... And the Word became flesh.
They crept up
stealthily, the Summer
grasses,
laying low all through
Spring like lily pads in a
lake of grey. Then, just
past the Solstice, when we
weren't looking, they broke
out in ambush, arresting
our gaze
with a swaying royal
purple which not even
Solomon,
in all his splendour, could
rival: we were surrounded.

Midsummer?

This morning, I thought I saw,
beneath grey skies,
the grasses grow
conspiratorial,
huddled in clumps,
perhaps plotting mayhem or
dreaming of dragonflies.

Parable

She went
seeking treasure
and found azure
hoards in a field
not even buried;
scattered,
not as husks
before swine
but as seeds
of glory,
droplets
of wine,
pearls
dislocated
from the seabed
purple-dyed
in his blood:

Harebells,
to ring in
the Kingdom

Harebells

Think of a colour
half violet, half sapphire,
a five-pointed star:
angular, rounded,
plump as a seaweed pod,
fine as a porcelain cup.
Harebells,
crouching on banks of grass,
amethyst manna in a desert land,
tinkling like coins on tarmac,
teetering on stalks
that make snowdrops' look clumpy,
or threaded in gorse
as bright Christmas lights,
soft flesh against spines:
intimations of mourning,
affirmations of love.

Late Summer Trilogy

In memoriam
Cliff Morgan, d. 29 August 2013
and Seamus Heaney, d. 30 August 2013

I THIS MESSAGE IS FLAGGED

Late August and the buddleia's
a-flutter with butterflies'
      w i n g s
opening and closing
like shutters to shield eyes
from the excess beauty
of light-catching things,
so many pennants
on the tents of eternity.

II ROWAN LANTERN

Already the rowan berries beam,
scarlet as billiard
balls against Summer's
green baize: branches weighed
down by ripe clusters
—choristers—
singing flesh into word.

III FLIGHT

And then they were gone.
We didn't catch when,
just sensed an absence
of movement; the pulse
of Summer
      slackened:
the swallows have flown.

To a Swallow

Freedom incarnate,
Summer's bright portent,
herald of Autumn,
fighter-pilot,
decimating sadness,
you'd rather
fly twelve thousand
miles than face a Winter.
Solar-powered,
charged with the glory of Spring,
your fleetness astonishes:
swifter than swifts,
graceful as a winged gazelle.
Yes, the heart stirs,
leaps, is left pinioned
beholding you, impossible
shard of life,
God's gymnast.
But oh, the thought of your flight
could leave us desolate
were we not
impelled by that
same urgent need
that drives the pilgrim.

Dear Swallow,
Godspeed;
Hasta la Vista!

Sunflower

Summer's ensign,
you signal weeks
of unfurled bliss;
flight from Winter's
iron grip. You span
God's unfolding plan:
bright May, solstice,
July's full and fiery kiss.
Striving still for the source
which drives you to the light,
you enflesh
singlemindedness,
while your radiance
stems the fast descending night.

How did your garden grow?

Surveying the balcony plot
this first day of Autumn
looking back through the thrum
of bees on a switch-back Summer
when the climate seemed sick
as the temperatures
rose and fell like
a fever
heat-waves rolling on cold snaps,
it was, you might say,
intemperate for England.

Vegetation sprouted like selvas
but no flowers or bees for weeks.
Only now, at the gate
to Winter,
as the days
shorten,
are set ablaze late
marigolds—three feet high—
and a rogue sunflower,
looking the sun in the eye,
questioning, as it pierces the sky.
It looks, you might say,
tropical for Yorkshire.

Autumn

Each year,
until you come,
I forget
your beauty,
as the face
of an absent friend:
that same ruddiness
that composure
of a still evening
waxing and waning
or crinkling
in laughter
like leaves
caught up by the wind
then masked by shade
so they fade
from memory.

Haikus

It's raining larch leaves,
bronze sparks struck from tinder box
bark, incandescent.

NOVEMBER
The woods, a war-zone
where stands sentinel Scots pine
watching for morning.

Autumn: The Sanctification of Leaves

Larch
English
gentle gold
like a lion's mane
potentially acidic
once spiky
now
mellowed
to
glory.

Birch,
Welsh,
fiery gold
from silver: alchemic
black branches of melancholy
turned to unalloyed
joy.

Scots
Pine
remaining
steadfastly
green.
Resisting change
until felled,
then
yielding
completely.

Irish
Hornbeams
sounding
almost too
rich a glow,
casting beams,
like Midas,
On all they touch.

Autumn at Crief

Each landscape has its season,
blossoms into speech:
Autumn is yours.
Now larch shows true hues
and birch leaves flicker
like sparks of a welder.
The last rays of light
skim the hill's brow
and fill Crief Gill
brimful of shades:
russets and old gold,
moving like madrigals
in a minor key.

Each landscape has its day,
speaks a word.
What do you say?
'Dry sticks can blaze;
dry bones can live.
Winter is deeply defeated.'

Felled

The forest neatly stacked to take away …

She walked, and found
a face revealed,
time told, once kept concealed
as kingly counsel:
this larch saw sixty-seven Summers.
Three score years and sev'n,
sensed Spring's sap's flow
wax incremental;
survived six decades
plus of Winter's trial.

Now felled, this larch lies
—unbranched—
as far from tree-like as
vertical from horizontal.
Yet,
witness of sixty-seven Easters,
bound to rise.

Better than Blackpool

When larch leans low igniting oak
with tapers tawny turning brown
and henna'd beech commiserates
with balding ash bereft of crown
and incandescent sycamore
welds hedges berried all ablaze
then God's illuminations show
his annual power to amaze.

All Saints—All Souls

Driving through the Forest of Compiègne
Overwhelmed by the sheer volume of leaves
Shed from beeches—so dense they might
Have grown not fallen—I wept.

Russet leaves, like spilt treasure, heaped against
Silver trunks, pierced by sudden green or snaking Aisne.
Leaves like souls touched by bright November light
Exposed, offering no resistance.

You spoke then of the searing pain in separation
As Somme's serried gravestones;
Speak now of resurrection and redemption
Speak a better word than Abel's blood.

Forest Fire in November

Braziers of bracken torch the larch branches gold.
Is this the kind of fire you came to start on earth
a copper pyre, a dance sparked by death
a holy conflagration to quicken hearts grown cold?
How I wish it were already ablaze.

Hourglass

(for A.J.)

Banded sands,
copper-aluminium,
skeins of time,
narrowing
as a life
empties
or fills
or prepares
to break the glass
to catch, on the rising tide,
eternity's fullness.

The Eve of St Hugh

Afternoon sun,
filtered
through larches,
makes redwoods
of the greenest stands:
a copper kingdom,
a Yorkshire Provence,
the song of a
troubadour
lost in the North,
singing his way to Spring.

To Christ the King

(after Cynewulf)

As we cross the perilous waters
of life, may you torch the way as a buoy,
fending off with your bow all foes.

Knowing our need
of the wealth of your kingship,
trading hardship for joy,
may we ride swiftly on steeds
of salvation and land safely
in your kingdom of peace.

Sabbath Rest

There'd been glimpses on the way:
headlands and shots of blue-grey between stone walls,
but the steep descent, narrow, devoid of vistas,
spoke more constraint than vision.
The stream—no more than a trickle—
promised little enough.

Nothing prepared us for the vastness,
the wideness—as mercy—the horizontal
temple of the sea,
shiny as gun-metal or shot satin;
the soul expanding to its full dimensions,
the body tranquil in its true element,
the spirit free in the sea of peace.

Last Post

In memoriam A.J. and J.A.J.

Just last week they were there,
a purple-headed troop,
a quiet triumph of the forest floor,
a rising fifth piercing the air
in plain, arresting beauty;
square-stemmed, labiate.
Could it be Ground Ivy?
I looked it up—
didn't google—
the white-striped lip
removed all doubt:
this was a clump of Bugle,
churned up now by
clumsy diggers' jaws
so the blooms lie dead in rows,
like Graves' remembered heroes,
recorded here as more
than vegetation:
a very present absence,
hope's registration.

Overwintering

In some ways
it wasn't the best place
to hibernate:
on the linen cupboard's
louvered doors,
your louvered wings
shut tight.

Perhaps you planned it thus?
For how many times, watching
these doors opening and
closing
on Winter's chores,
does the mind's eye
ignite
with a fore-flash of Spring's
full-throttled light,
and alight on those wings
opened right
out, bright against
darkness.

The Reaper

They were there for the taking:
Crisp, golden, unburied,
cast from above, set down in the yard,
a loose-leaved mound,
so that, shovel in hand
—strange reaper—
she might coax them into the gaping
mouth of a thin, black sack
which flapped
as a matador's winnowing cloak
until, like some prized swarm,
tight shut in a skep, that dead
leaf-hoard, harvest to come,
buzzed Spring in her step.

Maranatha

(for Illustrius)

You were sheer gift,
a kingfisher flash
out of the blue.
An answered prayer,
you shed grace
everywhere,
like an eastern potentate
dispensing alms.
For you, birches were palms:
the compost heap, a throne,
and where you walked,
high-stepped
and, yes, proud,
an arc of glory shone.

Notes and References

p. 2: 'The Birth of Christ', *Geni Crist* by Madog ap Gwallter
Madog ap Gwallter was a friar, probably Franciscan, a native of Llanfihangel Glyn Myfyr in Wales, who flourished in the middle of the thirteenth century.

The whole poem, some 64 lines long, is a joyful proclamation of the birth of Christ who has come to us not in majesty but as a child.

Whether the poet was a Franciscan or not, the poem certainly has the hallmark of homely Franciscan simplicity which cannot have failed to have roused his hearers when delivered in the vernacular Welsh tongue and in the culturally sympathetic form of poetry.

While the original verses are set out in *rhupunt* metre, each line comprising three phrases, this version attempts to capture something of the triadic structure by the use of triplets.

This translation draws on the Welsh text of the *Oxford Book of Welsh Verse*, ed. Thomas Parry (1962), as well as from the now standard version of the Poets of the Princes series produced by the University of Wales Centre for Advanced Studies, vol. vii, *Gwaith Bleddyn Fardd a Beirdd Eraill Ail Hanner y Drydedd Ganrif ar Ddeg*, ed. Rhian M. Andrews *et al.* (Cardiff, 1999).

p. 6: 'The Herald'
The first line, 'This star burns', is taken from the fourth antiphon of Vespers for Epiphany, *Stella ista coruscat.*

p. 16: 'Behold the Man'
Based on John 9.

p. 19: 'Mary Reflects'
This poem was read by Jennifer Chisholm in King's College Chapel, Cambridge, for their 'Carols from King's' service on 9 December 2018 and filmed by the BBC for television on Christmas Eve.

p. 21: 'Lily-Cricifix'
line 5: *nephesh*: the Hebrew carries the meaning of 'breath'; cf. Genesis 2:7.

p. 24: 'Maundy Daffodils'
last line: the quotation is from George Mackay Brown, 'Song for
St Magnus', 1993.

pp. 29–37: *Cadentine Rites*
This sequence of poems follows the events of Holy Week in
dialogue with the Latin Ferial Vespers hymns from the ancient
Monastic Antiphoner as they move between accounts of the first
creation in Genesis and the new creation ushered in by Christ's
Paschal Mystery.

Written during the Community's last Holy Week at Stanbrook
Abbey, Worcester, in 2009, an earlier version of the sequence was
hand-set and printed by the Evergreen Press in a limited edition
in 2012 as a thanksgiving to God for bringing the Community
safely through the move to Yorkshire.

p. 39: 'A hart can never . . .': title from George Herbert's 'Easter'.

p. 43: 'Wass Peacock'
The opening citation is from Psalm 112/113: 7–8, translated from
the Vulgate by the author.
line 7: Ezekiel's vision is found in Ezekiel 37.
line 11: 'long pinions unfurling 'neath a mastering blue': cf. 'A
Windy Day in Summer' by Gerard Manley Hopkins.
line 15: For the 'Julian shewing' here, cf. *Revelations of Divine Love*
by Julian of Norwich, ch. 51.

p. 48: 'Not even Solomon'
'All flesh is grass' Isaiah 40: 6
'And the Word became flesh . . .' John: Prologue 14.

p. 64: 'Forest Fire in November'
Last line, Luke 12: 49.

p. 67: 'To Christ the King' (after Cynewulf)
In 1840, the Danish scholar N. S. F. Grundtvig discovered the name
of Cynewulf 'signed' in runes within several medieval poems. As
well as standing for letters, which in this case spell out 'Cynewulf',
runes can also signify objects. So, for example: the rune ᚳ for 'C'
= 'torch', ᚣ for 'Y' = 'bow; ᚾ for 'N', 'need/hardship'; ᛖ for 'E',
'steed'; ᚹ for 'W', 'joy'; ᚢ for 'U', 'our'; ᛚ for 'L', 'water'; ᚠ for 'F',
'wealth'. The poem makes use of all the runes which make up
Cynewulf's name.

9 780852 449653